Revolutionary War Leaders

John Hancock

President of the Continental Congress

Colonial Leaders

Lord Baltimore
English Politician and Colonist

Benjamin Banneker
American Mathematician and Astronomer

Sir William Berkeley
Governor of Virginia

William Bradford
Governor of Plymouth Colony

Jonathan Edwards
Colonial Religious Leader

Benjamin Franklin
American Statesman, Scientist, and Writer

Anne Hutchinson
Religious Leader

Cotton Mather
Author, Clergyman, and Scholar

Increase Mather
Clergyman and Scholar

James Oglethorpe
Humanitarian and Soldier

William Penn
Founder of Democracy

Sir Walter Raleigh
English Explorer and Author

Caesar Rodney
American Patriot

John Smith
English Explorer and Colonist

Miles Standish
Plymouth Colony Leader

Peter Stuyvesant
Dutch Military Leader

George Whitefield
Clergyman and Scholar

Roger Williams
Founder of Rhode Island

John Winthrop
Politician and Statesman

John Peter Zenger
Free Press Advocate

Revolutionary War Leaders

John Adams
Second U.S. President

Ethan Allen
Revolutionary Hero

Benedict Arnold
Traitor to the Cause

King George III
English Monarch

Nathanael Greene
Military Leader

Nathan Hale
Revolutionary Hero

Alexander Hamilton
First U.S. Secretary of the Treasury

John Hancock
President of the Continental Congress

Patrick Henry
American Statesman and Speaker

John Jay
First Chief Justice of the Supreme Court

Thomas Jefferson
Author of the Declaration of Independence

John Paul Jones
Father of the U.S. Navy

Lafayette
French Freedom Fighter

James Madison
Father of the Constitution

Francis Marion
The Swamp Fox

James Monroe
American Statesman

Thomas Paine
Political Writer

Paul Revere
American Patriot

Betsy Ross
American Patriot

George Washington
First U.S. President

Famous Figures of the Civil War Era

Jefferson Davis
Confederate President

Frederick Douglass
Abolitionist and Author

Ulysses S. Grant
Military Leader and President

Stonewall Jackson
Confederate General

Robert E. Lee
Confederate General

Abraham Lincoln
Civil War President

William Sherman
Union General

Harriet Beecher Stowe
Author of Uncle Tom's Cabin

Sojourner Truth
Abolitionist, Suffragist, and Preacher

Harriet Tubman
Leader of the Underground Railroad

Revolutionary War Leaders

John Hancock

President of the Continental Congress

Ann Graham Gaines

Arthur M. Schlesinger, jr.
Senior Consulting Editor

Chelsea House Publishers

Philadelphia

Produced by 21st Century Publishing and Communications, Inc.
New York, NY. http://www.21cpc.com

CHELSEA HOUSE PUBLISHERS
Production Manager Pamela Loos
Art Director Sara Davis
Director of Photography Judy L. Hasday
Managing Editor James D. Gallagher
Senior Production Editor J. Christopher Higgins

Staff for ***JOHN HANCOCK***
Project Editor/Publishing Coordinator Jim McAvoy
Project Editor Anne Hill
Associate Art Director Takeshi Takahashi
Series Design Keith Trego

The Chelsea House World Wide Web address is
http://www.chelseahouse.com

First Printing
1 3 5 7 9 8 6 4 2

Library of Congress Cataloging-in-Publication Data

Gaines, Ann.
John Hancock / Ann G. Gaines.
p. cm. — (Revolutionary War leaders)
Includes bibliographical references and index.
ISBN 0-7910-5975-8 (hc) — 0-7910-6133-7 (pbk.)
1. Hancock, John, 1737-1793—Juvenile literature. 2. Statemen—United States—Biography—Juvenile literature. 3. United States. Declaration of Independence—Signers—Biography—Juvenile literature. 4. United States—History—Revolution, 1775-1783—Juvenile literature. [1. Hancock, John, 1737-1793. 2. Statemen. 3. United States—History—Revolution, 1775-1783.] I. Title. II. Series.

E302.6.H23 G35 2000
973.3'092—dc21
[B] 00-038391
CIP

Publisher's Note: In Colonial and Revolutionary War America, there were no standard rules for spelling, punctuation, capitalization, or grammar. Some of the quotations that appear in the Colonial Leaders and Revolutionary War Leaders series come from original documents and letters written during this time in history. Original quotations reflect writing inconsistencies of the period.

Contents

A busy Boston street in the time of John Hancock. When John was a boy, he moved to Boston to live with his uncle, a rich merchant.

1

Early Life

John Hancock differed from most other American Revolutionary War leaders because he was very rich. He was a **merchant** and a politician. After years in the **legislature** of the **colony** of Massachusetts, he became president of the Second Continental Congress. Later he was the first governor of the new state of Massachusetts. Today, he is best remembered as the first signer of the Declaration of Independence.

John's **ancestors** came to the New World from England and had settled in the Massachusetts Bay Colony by 1648. The Hancock family prospered and soon became one of Massachusetts's powerful families.

John's father and grandfather were also named John Hancock. His grandfather graduated from Harvard College and moved to Lexington, Massachusetts, where he became a minister. John's father also went to Harvard and then entered the ministry. John's father was a friendly man. In 1733, he married Mary Hawke Thaxter. Two years later, they had their first child, Mary. Next their son, John, was born, on January 12, 1737. In 1741, they had another son, Ebenezer.

Johnny, as the boy was known, was a happy child. His parents were well-off. Townspeople respected his father. At five, Johnny went to a dame school, which was like a kindergarten, to learn his ABCs and easy sums. Then he went to a regular school for older children.

Johnny's father wanted him to follow in his footsteps. Johnny was expected to go to Harvard and then become a minister, too. But these plans changed after his father died in 1744. In those days, women did not usually hold jobs. The death of her husband left Johnny's mother without an

John Hancock, his father, and his grandfather were all graduates of Harvard College, one of the first schools established in America.

income to support her family. The family had to move in with Johnny's grandfather in Lexington.

Johnny did not live in Lexington long. In 1745, at age eight, he left his family and went to live with Thomas Hancock, his uncle. Thomas Hancock was a merchant in the bustling port city of Boston. He never went to college but started out as an **apprentice** bookbinder. By the time

Johnny came to live with him, he was a rich man. He owned a store, ships, and an elegant house on Beacon Hill. He and his wife, Lydia, had no children. They welcomed Johnny and always treated him kindly. Thomas hoped one day Johnny would join him in his business.

Beacon Hill was one of three hills that sat above central Boston. When Thomas and Lydia Hancock became rich, they wanted to move out of the crowded part of town. They bought a large parcel of land on Beacon Hill, on which they built an elegant mansion. It had more than 20 rooms and was surrounded by fancy gardens. In the years that followed, other rich people would build their houses on Beacon Hill. Today it remains a very fashionable place to live and is recognized as a historic district.

Johnny liked life in Boston. One of the largest cities in the colonies, it was a very exciting place. There, he enrolled in the Latin School, studying Latin, Greek, history, philosophy, and **theology**. One hour a day he went to a special "writing school," where he learned reading, writing, spelling, and arithmetic.

Johnny was just an average student. Nevertheless, in five years he had learned all he could at the Latin School. By this time, Thomas Hancock had been elected a selectman, a member of the town council. At the same time, he made a great deal of money from contracts with the British government. The British were fighting a war against the French and the Spanish to control the colonies in America and their army needed food, clothes, and ammunition, which Thomas Hancock happily sold to them. Johnny heard many stories of heroic deeds by British soldiers, and he dreamed of one day being a soldier.

In the fall of 1750, he enrolled at Harvard College. John, as he was now called, was 13 years old. He studied Latin, Greek, Hebrew, and philosophy. The school had recently added some new courses, including geography, geometry, and astronomy, but offered no classes in history or politics. He learned about these things by reading Greek and Roman history.

John graduated in 1754 and went back to live

In 1650, Boston, Massachusetts, was the largest town in the colonies. One hundred years later, Philadelphia and New York were bigger. But Boston, with a population of 16,000 people, still bustled. The city hugged a harbor. Many ships docked at its wharves; warehouses and shops lined them. On higher ground were shops, offices, markets, and houses. Many of Boston's buildings were built of brick. In the center of town was Boston Common. Because Boston was the capital of the Massachusetts Bay Colony, the governor lived there. The colonial legislature met there in the state house.

with his uncle, who had become more powerful in Massachusetts politics. He was appointed to the Governor's Council, meaning he advised the royal governor of Massachusetts. He had less time for the business and turned to John for help. John agreed to work with him. Thomas taught John all about importing and exporting goods. They visited the shops and warehouses. At the docks, John talked to the captains of ships that were owned by the Hancock family.

By 1759, John played a large role in the business. The next year, Thomas showed how much he trusted John by sending him to London on a business trip. John stayed there for a year,

Sailing ships in the busy port of London. John spent about a year in London negotiating big contracts and making business deals for his uncle's company.

negotiating new contracts with merchants and bankers. He returned home in July 1761. His uncle was very pleased with the deals John had made in London. On January 1, 1763, Thomas made John his full partner. At that time, they expected to run their business together for many years. But this was not to be. On August 1, 1764, Thomas died unexpectedly.

As a young man, John Hancock followed the fashion of the times; he wore shirts with ruffled sleeves and a powdered white wig, as shown in his portrait.

2

In Business

When Thomas Hancock died, the people of Boston found out that he had been even wealthier than they had thought. He had started with nothing, but as a result of hard work had amassed a great fortune. In his will, he remembered many people. His wife, Lydia Hancock, inherited land, money, and their house with its fancy furnishings. He provided for his sisters, nieces, nephews, slaves, and friends. Although he had not gone to Harvard, he left the college enough money to hire a new professor of Asian languages. The town of Boston received enough money to build a hospital for its mentally ill citizens.

John inherited more from his uncle than anybody else. Thomas had owned 22,000 acres of land in Boston, elsewhere in Massachusetts, and in Maine. John got the best pieces, including a lot of valuable **real estate** in Boston. He also inherited Thomas's entire business, including his shops, warehouses, inventory, and ships. By today's standards, John would be a millionaire.

His uncle's death made John not only one of Boston's wealthiest merchants, but also the master of an elegant mansion. A week after Thomas was buried, Lydia signed the house she had inherited over to John. She lived there for the rest of her days. It turned out to be a happy arrangement. Until John married, Lydia ran his household, telling the servants what to do and the cook what to serve.

John enjoyed his new life. Portraits of him as a young man show he was handsome and slim, though not very tall. He had dark brown hair, but in the style of the day he usually wore a powdered wig of short, white hair. John was a stylish dresser. He wore ruffled shirts and suits made especially for him from velvet and other fancy fabrics which were decorated with gold trim.

Like other men in his family, John did not marry until later in life. Society considered him a very eligible bachelor; many rich women would have been pleased to marry him. He loved to throw lavish parties. As a member of many social clubs, he also received many invitations to parties.

It was easy for John to become completely responsible for the business he and his uncle had run together. He paid it a great deal of attention. His ships carried raw products like **potash**, whale oil, and timber to Europe. Once his captains sold these goods, they bought other fancy goods like fabric and spices and brought them back to Boston for John to sell.

The Hancock business continued to grow, and John made money in other ways, too. He

John Hancock's ships were huge wooden vessels. They had three tall masts (a tall one in the front, the tallest in the middle, and the shortest at the back). The masts' rigging carried huge sails that could be raised or lowered. Wind filled the sails, moving the ships. Sailing ships could carry people, animals, or cargo. Cargo was carefully loaded into ships' holds. It had to be balanced and could not move. There was usually just one cabin, which was for the captain. A ship needed a large crew. John's ships went to sea for weeks at a time.

bought real estate and set up his brother, Ebenezer, with a hardware store.

But soon merchants all over the American colonies began to lose money. In the **mother country**–Britain–the economy was in trouble. Britain had won the Seven Years' War in Europe, which was called the French and Indian War in America, and the victory meant that the British gained control over the vast lands of Canada from the French. But Britain had borrowed a lot of money to fight the war. When the war ended, Britain had a large national debt. Also, gaining all that new land meant they needed more money because they had to set up new colonial governments and pay soldiers to

Large sailing ships such as these were important to John's business. They carried cargo to other countries and brought back goods to be sold in Boston.

protect these new colonies.

To solve its money problems, Britain started to tax its citizens who lived in the American colonies. British citizens in England already paid high taxes. For years, the colonists in America had paid no taxes.

Many in America claimed that because the colonists had no representatives in the British **Parliament**, they should not be taxed at all. Parliament wanted to force the American colonies to recognize its right to tax them, so they passed the Sugar Act in 1762.

The act increased the **duty** Americans paid on molasses, which they used to make rum. The act also said that American traders had to ship raw materials like lumber, iron, and furs to Britain. They could no longer trade directly with other European countries like the Netherlands. Captains were required to fill out a lot of paperwork regarding their cargo. If they did not do so, their ships could be seized.

These new restrictions on trade meant that John earned less money. He remained very rich, but he was still worried. In a letter to some friends in Britain he complained, "no vessel hardly comes in or goes out but they find some pretense to seize and detain her."

At that time the colonists did not organize to protest the act. John, for one, was not yet interested in political protest. He complained about the act's effect on his business, but did not see a serious problem in the relationship between the colonies and the British government.

This soon changed. In March 1765, at age 28, John was elected to the office of selectman for the town of Boston. He became one of five members of the town board, which made local laws and controlled Boston's budget.

Within weeks of his election, Parliament passed the Stamp Act, which was designed to collect more revenues from the colonies. This new law said a special stamp had to be used on all legal and business documents. The government collected a little money every time a colonist bought a newspaper, got a professional license, bought a piece of land, or drew up a will.

This time, leaders of the colonies protested to

Parliament before the act became law, but they were ignored. John hoped Parliament would **rescind** the act before it went into effect on November 1. If not, he wrote, "we must submit."

But not all the colonists agreed. Patrick Henry, a lawyer and politician from the Virginia colony, gave a speech in which he said that only the legislatures in the colonies themselves could tax the colonists.

Copies of Henry's speech circulated through the colonies. Many people agreed with him. By this time, John had become friends with a group of Massachusetts politicians who would soon become revolutionaries. Samuel Adams was one of them. John listened to Adams talk of how unfairly England treated its colonies.

People in Boston had begun protesting the Stamp Act before it went into effect. A secret society named the Sons of Liberty was formed and started taking action.

One August morning, an **effigy** of Andrew Oliver, the stamp master, swung from a tree.

Samuel Adams was one of the founders of the Sons of Liberty. He would later sign the Declaration of Independence.

That night, a mob tore down a building Oliver owned. When the mob started to march toward his house, his family fled. The mob totally wrecked their home. The next day, John spoke out. He did not want Oliver to get hurt, but he understood the mob's anger. He no longer thought the colonies should submit. Now he was in favor of resistance.

Less than two weeks later, another mob rioted and destroyed the home of the lieutenant governor of Massachusetts. Once again, John protested the violence. He did not like violence at all. He preferred other, more peaceful, forms of protest. John did join Samuel Adams's Liberty Party, a group of men interested in politics who would become more devoted to the cause of liberty and eventually work for the independence of the American colonies.

As the date the Stamp Act would go into effect approached, John complained more and more. In mid-October, he wrote, "I have come to a serious Resolution not to send one Ship more to sea nor to have any kind of Connection in Business under a Stamp." He and other Boston merchants signed an agreement not to

John had a very successful shipping business. But he decided not to import goods from Great Britain in protest of the hated British stamp tax.

import certain goods from Britain. He began to build his own reputation as a **patriot**.

Rumors that the hated Stamp Act would be

repealed soon flew around Boston. John began to place orders for goods, believing the rumors would turn out to be true. And indeed, it seemed as if they were. On April 17, 1766, a local newspaper unofficially reported the Stamp Act would be repealed.

Not long thereafter, Samuel Adams asked John to consider running for a seat in the colonial legislature. John agreed and on May 6, he won the election.

On May 16, 1766, official news of the repeal of the Stamp Tax came from Britain. The town of Boston celebrated in grand style. John had his servants put lanterns in each of his mansion's 54 windows.

He also "gave a grand and elegant Entertainment to the genteel Part of the Town," inviting other rich people to a banquet. But while he did not invite working-class people into his home, he made sure they had plenty to drink. In front of his house, he installed a fountain that spouted wine. He also paid for the Sons of Liberty's magnificent fireworks display.

John continued to run his business for a few more years. But politics consumed more and more of his free time. Sometimes he missed town council meetings, but he worked hard in the colonial legislature. After the Stamp Act was repealed, colonists expressed their gratitude to the British Parliament and the king, sending them messages of thanks. The Sons of Liberty ceased to meet. Colonists were proud again that they were part of the British empire. But a new crisis was fast approaching.

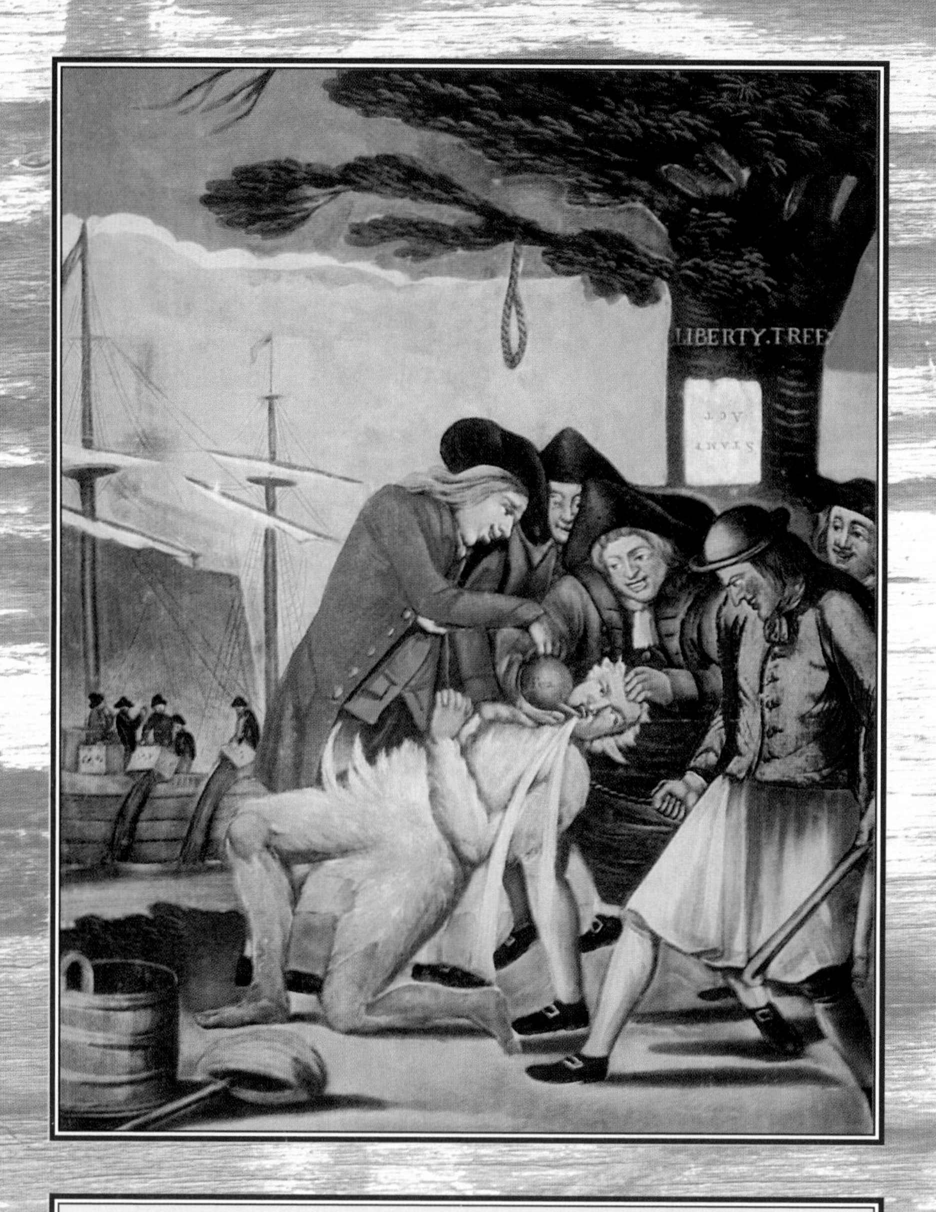

A British cartoon shows angry colonists pouring tea down the throat of a British tax collector, who also has been tarred and feathered. In the background, other colonists are dumping tea from British ships into the harbor.

3

Revolution!

After the Stamp Act was repealed in 1766, life in Boston quieted down. John spent time in his shops and warehouses and on the wharves, tending to his business. Two of his ships sailed back and forth between Boston and London, carrying cargo and passengers. He also owned shares in other ships. On February 19, 1767, he made one of his biggest deals ever–he bought a wharf. There was only one wharf in the harbor that had more berths for ships. John expected to make a lot of money. He charged ships a fee for docking there. He also owned the buildings along his wharf and collected rent from the dozen storekeepers who had shops in them.

In March 1767, John was reelected to both Boston's town board and the colonial legislature. Except for the Stamp Act affair, politics had become pretty dull. Legislators had some arguments with the governor, but mostly they just attended to the business of running the colony.

Soon Americans would once more have reason to rebel against the mother country. The king appointed Charles Townshend to be the new chancellor of the Exchequer, the British treasury. Townshend turned his attention to the old problem of how to raise money to pay for the British soldiers in America.

During the protests against the Stamp Act, the colonists had argued that it was unfair for Parliament to collect taxes from business that was conducted only in the colonies. Parliament had agreed. But Townshend believed it would be fair for Parliament to collect duties on goods that came to the colonies from outside. Townshend's

Revenue Act of 1767 meant colonists were going to have to pay extra for glass, paint, lead, paper, and tea. These were things the colonists needed that had to be imported from abroad.

One thing Townshend wanted to do with the money collected was to take over the paying of salaries of colonial governors and other officials. In the past, colonial legislatures had paid them, and sometimes the legislatures refused to pay a man who would not do what they wanted. Townshend hoped to take that control away from colonists. The Townshend Act never actually collected a lot of money. But that was all right with the members of Parliament. What they really wanted to do was to demonstrate their right to tax the colonists.

John complained to his friends and neighbors about the new taxes on imported goods. He also wrote letters to people he knew in London. In October, some citizens of Boston agreed among themselves that after the new year they would import less. They would lead simple lives, without

British warships arrive at Boston Harbor to protect British interests in the American colonies. In 1768 a British warship seized one of John's ships, and he was charged with smuggling.

purchasing many luxuries. John went along with this mild protest. For John and others, it was not that the taxes themselves were so bad, it was more that Britain, 3,000 miles away, was again passing taxes on their American colonies when there were no American representatives in Parliament.

Resistance to the Townshend Act became

widespread throughout the colonies. At a meeting of the Massachusetts legislature, John encouraged everyone to work to produce glass, lead, paint, and other products so that the colonies would not have to import those things. At the request of the legislature, Samuel Adams circulated a letter throughout the colonies. The letter **condemned** Britain and all taxation without representation. Most other colonial legislatures refused to vote in support of the letter, but it still alarmed British officials.

In the meantime, John had been making changes in his business. He cut off ties with the firm in London with which he had done the most business. He began to do business only with firms that supported the colonies and opposed the king and Parliament. In February, John got in trouble with the British governor, who asked Parliament to condemn a newspaper article that seemed to criticize him. Parliament would not do as the governor asked and sent John to tell him that freedom of the press had to be maintained.

On March 14, 1768, John was reelected as a selectman. During the same period, he and other merchants put together a new agreement concerning goods they would not import. Citizens hung more officials in effigy and threatened customs commissioners. Violence began to break out in Boston. John was never seen among the Sons of Liberty, but he supported them.

Soon John found himself in more trouble. He was rich enough that when taxes seemed likely to hurt his business, he simply stopped trading in taxed goods. But British officials decided he must be smuggling because he remained so rich. The local British commissioners watched his ships come and go. On April 8, 1768, officials boarded and seized his ship, the *Lydia.* But the attorney general made them release the ship because, he said, the search was illegal.

On May 4, 1768, John was again reelected to the legislature. Its members chose him to serve as one of their advisors to the governor.

But the governor refused to accept him as a member of his council.

Then he got in trouble once again. Another of his ships, the *Liberty*, arrived in port and a customs official came to inspect its cargo. The crew threw him into a cabin and nailed it shut. Then they hurriedly unloaded its illegal cargo–wine from Portugal. The official was finally released. But this whole affair angered the British officials so much that they decided to charge John with smuggling, and they seized the *Liberty*.

The HMS *Romney*, a British warship armed with 50 cannons, sailed into Boston Harbor. Its sailors rowed a boat over and threw a rope onto the *Liberty*, then towed the ship over to the *Romney*. A huge crowd of townspeople gathered to watch. Angered, they became violent, smashing windows along the wharf and setting a tax collector's small boat on fire. The British commissioners fled Boston because they were afraid for their lives. John did not take part in the violence, but he enjoyed what the mob had done. On August 17, 1768, the British judge ruled that the *Liberty* would be put up for sale.

By this time, Charles Townshend had died. But the King of Britain had created another new position–secretary of state for the colonies. Lord Hillsborough was selected for the job.

Hillsborough became very angry over Samuel Adams's circular that called the Townshend Acts unfair. He ordered the Massachusetts legislature to take back the circular. He also ordered the legislatures of the other colonies to refuse to endorse it. Hillsborough further ordered colonial governors to dissolve any legislatures that refused to carry out his orders.

John and his fellow legislators in Massachusetts voted not to take back the circular and then adjourned. When the governor's order came for the legislature to dissolve, no one was there.

Until this time, John had been just one of many members of the radical political group. But after the *Liberty* affair, he became a hero. Colonists regarded him as a revolutionary leader. In August 1768, he and other merchants agreed they would import virtually nothing from Britain for one year–from January 1, 1769, to January 1, 1770. Coal, gunpowder, and gunshot would be all they would ship in. They would not buy tea, paper, glass, or paint until the Townshend Acts were repealed.

John became convinced that the American colonies needed to break off from the mother country. His business was doing very poorly. He sold oil and potash abroad, but his ships returned to Boston empty because he refused to import anything for which he would have to pay taxes. He did do a little money lending. John also engaged in a flurry of political activities, serving in his elected capacities and going to secret meetings with fellow revolutionaries.

He came into conflict many times with the British governor, Francis Bernard, and protested the arrival of British troops in Boston in October 1768. Then a New York newspaper published a series of articles describing what was happening in Boston, and John was portrayed as liberty's protector. In November, John was arrested on charges of importing goods without paying taxes on them. Some friends put up bail for him. John Adams, another revolutionary, acted as his lawyer and got the case dropped.

To remove the legislature from the influence of Boston revolutionaries, Governor Bernard ordered the members to leave Boston and start meeting in Cambridge, which is across the harbor. The representatives went to the meeting but still would not cooperate with the British officials. Infuriated, Bernard ordered them to adjourn the session once more.

Over the next couple of years, the situation continued to get worse. Colonists were fighting back against the British control more and more. There were even open conflicts with British soldiers in the streets. On March 5, 1770, British troops fired into a mob of colonists in Boston, killing five and wounding eight. Samuel

A dramatic drawing by Paul Revere, showing British soldiers firing on unarmed citizens of Boston. Samuel Adams called this event the "Boston Massacre."

Adams labeled the event a massacre. John was one of the committee of Boston residents who demanded that the British troops be withdrawn from the city after the Boston Massacre.

Britain decided to stop collecting most of the hated taxes but kept the tax on tea. Tea was a popular drink in the colonies. The colonists did not want to do without their favorite drink and began to buy large quantities of Dutch tea that was smuggled into the colonies. In May 1773, Parliament passed the Tea Act, which reduced the price of taxed English tea to less than the price of smuggled Dutch tea without the tax. The British felt that the colonists would give in and pay the hated tax in order to get the cheaper tea.

They were wrong. In December 1773, John helped Samuel Adams organize the Boston Tea Party. On the night of December 16, about 150 men dressed as American Indians boarded three British ships which had just arrived in Boston and dumped more than 300 chests of British tea into Boston Harbor. In response, the British closed the harbor to all traffic and sent even more soldiers to patrol the colony. Open warfare seemed to be quickly approaching.

Some angry colonists disguised themselves as American Indians and dumped 300 chests of British tea into Boston Harbor. This event became known as the Boston Tea Party.

In 1774, John cut his last ties with the British government. For years, he had commanded the Massachusetts First Corps of Cadets, a military group that served the British governor as a bodyguard. After a quarrel with the new colonial governor, Thomas Gage, John quit his command and openly encouraged rebellion.

John and his wife, Dolly. Soon after their marriage, the couple moved to Philadelphia, where John served as president of the Second Continental Congress.

4

Helping to Build a New Nation

By nature, John was a proud and flamboyant man. Over the years, he offended many with his sharp tongue. But he also came through, over and over again, for the American cause, doing all he could to help the patriots succeed. On March 5, 1774, John gave the annual Massacre Day oration to the citizens of Boston. In his speech, he proposed that delegates from every colony come together to establish a Congress. His idea caught on, and the First Continental Congress was called. John was not one of the representatives who rode to Philadelphia for its meeting. By this time, he had begun to suffer from a painful disease called gout that made moving about very uncomfortable.

There was plenty for him to do in Boston. A change was occurring in his personal life. He had begun to court a woman named Dolly Quincy. Things continued to happen on the political scene, too. On October 5, 1774, the legislature was scheduled to meet. But at the last moment, Governor Gage canceled the meeting. The members of the legislature disobeyed Gage's order and met anyway. When the governor failed to come to the meeting, the representatives voted to become a convention.

The very next day, the convention voted to become the Provisional Congress, and John was elected its first president. The people of Massachusetts finally had an independent government of their own, which would not answer to the king of Britain.

The Provisional Congress met all fall and winter, first in Concord and then in Cambridge. They started to collect taxes to support their cause. On October 29, they voted to create companies of soldiers called "minutemen" who would be ready for action at a moment's notice. The companies of minutemen were created by assembling groups from each colony's militia.

On December 1, John was elected a delegate to the Second Continental Congress, which was scheduled to meet the next spring. When the Provincial Congress adjourned, John went home to Beacon Hill. Boston had become a dangerous town. A lot of people who were still loyal to the British government were moving into the town from the surrounding areas, seeking the protection of the British soldiers stationed there.

In February 1775, the Massachusetts Provisional Congress began meeting again and reelected John president. He also served as a member of the town's Committee of Safety and as a town selectman. His influence was huge. He was working as a full-time politician and was doing virtually no business. He was spending all of his time and energy working exclusively for the American colonies.

At one point, the British government had wanted John Hancock and Samuel Adams arrested and brought to Britain for a trial. But Governor Gage, fearing trouble, would not do so. John returned to the Provisional Congress, which turned its attention to drawing up regulations for a Massachusetts army. He knew that it was just a matter of time before the British government would try to stop him again. In the spring of 1775, he sold his last ships and sent his aunt and Dolly Quincy to Lexington in case there was trouble in Boston.

A week later, Governor Gage decided to act. He had learned from a spy that the colonists were hiding guns and ammunition in Concord, a nearby town. Samuel Adams and John Hancock were also in Concord, at the Provisional Congress. Gage decided to send troops there to arrest the two men and seize the guns and ammunition. But Paul Revere, head of a group of American spies, was determined to warn the Provisional Congress of Gage's plan. On April 18, 1775,

During Paul Revere's famous ride, the American spy warned people that British troops were coming.

when the British troops started to move toward Concord, Revere made his famous ride, warning the colonists along the way: "The British are coming! The British are coming!"

By the time the unsuspecting British army

Battles at Lexington, and at Concord's North Bridge (shown here), were the first armed confrontations between the colonists and the British and marked the beginning of the American Revolutionary War.

reached Lexington, on the way to Concord, fierce fighting broke out. In a face-to-face battle on the square, men on both sides were killed. The British army continued its march to Concord. There, the British destroyed some of the colonists' gunpowder and supplies. During the march back to Boston, the British troops were attacked by snipers hiding behind stone walls and fences. This marked the beginning of the American Revolution. After these terrible and bloody battles, there was no way to turn back.

John and Samuel Adams fled north from Concord and got away without being captured by the British soldiers. They met up with Lydia and Dolly in Woburn, and together headed for Worcester, Massachusetts, where they thought they would meet other delegates of the Continental Congress. But in Worcester, they found no delegates and no word from Congress.

John wrote to the Committee of Safety, whose members immediately sent him a military escort. Soon the other expected delegates arrived. John sent the women to Fairfield, Connecticut, where they would stay with a friend in safety. A few days later, John left Worcester, bound for New York City. There, a crowd numbering more than 5,000 people turned out to see his carriage go by. Four days later he arrived in Philadelphia. As he entered the city, crowds gathered to cheer there as well.

The Second Continental Congress began that very day. Thomas Jefferson from Virginia, Benjamin Franklin from Pennsylvania, and John from Massachusetts were its most famous new members.

Thousands of colonial militiamen had turned out to surround Boston. More fighting could break out at any time. The new Congress spent its first days discussing what had happened so far. They knew a full-blown war was almost certainly coming. On May 24, the Congress had to elect a new president. Peyton Randolph had been its president, but he needed to go home because of bad health. John was elected by a unanimous vote to replace Randolph.

On June 2, the Continental Congress received a letter from Joseph Warren, the new president of the Massachusetts Provincial Congress, asking what they should do about the British army. Warren wanted the Continental Congress to take charge of the matter. The Continental Congress

George Washington leads the colonial army in battle against the British. John had hoped to be chosen general, but Washington had more combat experience and was selected for the position instead.

voted to accept the responsibility and the Continental Army was formed in response. Next, the Congress had to find a general for the new army. John hoped that he would get the job. He had been a militia commander, and he believed that he was a good leader. But he had no combat experience and George Washington was chosen instead.

John admired Washington. As president of the Second Continental Congress, John had a very important role to play as well. He shaped events and influenced decisions. It was his job to make the delegates work together. One of his greatest contributions to the Congress was money. He contributed whatever he could. Some of it went to pay the new government's expenses, but most of it went to buy guns, ammunition, and supplies for the army.

On June 12, 1775, General Gage offered the rebellious colonists peace. But he singled out Samuel Adams and John Hancock, saying they had to be punished. The two men felt that this was an honor. Five days later came the Battle of Bunker Hill. More than 1,000 British soldiers were killed or wounded by the American colonial soldiers, the worst **casualty** rate the British army had ever suffered.

The Battle of Bunker Hill was an important early battle fought near Boston. The British suffered a terrible defeat with more than 1,000 British soldiers being killed or wounded in one day.

The news reached Philadelphia on June 24, and 100 people gathered at John's house to hear the details. At one o'clock in the morning, John, Samuel Adams, and John Adams sent a message to the Philadelphia Committee of Safety, asking that gunpowder be sent to the colonists who were fighting in Massachusetts.

At this time, some colonists still hoped to avoid war with the British. John was not one of them, but he made sure all points of view were heard in Congress. Delegates liked him. He kept up a frantic pace, frequently getting extremely tired. His eyes bothered him, so he started wearing glasses. On August 1, Congress adjourned.

John was on his way out of town within hours. He went right to see Dolly Quincy. They set August 28 as their wedding day. John then left on a short trip to Boston. He found his business was in ruins. His business manager had not been able to trade for him or buy real estate. He also found that his **mansion** was in enemy hands, and there was nothing that he could do about it. John returned to Fairfield for his wedding.

After they were married, John and his new

bride traveled to Philadelphia where they found a nice home in which to settle down. The mood was somber across the colonies, as people realized what it meant to be at war with Britain. But John and Dolly found married life much to their liking, and for the time, they were very happy.

Soon the Continental Congress met in a new session. It issued orders to the army, set up a post office, negotiated treaties with Native Americans, and borrowed money. But conflict arose between John, Samuel Adams, and John Adams. The three men disagreed as to which branch of the Massachusetts legislature had the right to appoint militia officers, with John alone in his position. What started out as a small argument soon caused a permanent break between the friends.

As president of the Continental Congress, John worked six days a week. He did a lot of paperwork, and attended many committee meetings and general sessions of Congress. Often the committees met at 7 A.M.; general sessions lasted

Members of the committee, including John Adams, Thomas Jefferson, and Benjamin Franklin, present the Declaration of Independence to John (seated, far right), the president of the Continental Congress.

from 10 A.M. to 5 P.M.; and committees often met again until 10 P.M. John presided over the general sessions. He also reviewed and signed all official documents. He had very little time to give to his business, which continued to suffer. But his marriage continued to bring him great joy. He and Dolly entertained often, despite being short of cash. In March 1776, the British left Boston and British General Henry Clinton moved out of John's mansion.

In May of the same year, John received word that he had been elected general of the Massachusetts militia. In the meantime, the Continental Congress was meeting and debating whether they should formally declare America's independence from Britain. On July 1, Congress appointed an important committee to prepare a declaration of independence. John Adams, Benjamin Franklin, and Thomas Jefferson were on the committee.

How did Americans first learn of the Declaration of Independence? Messengers carried copies of the document all over the colonies. It was read aloud to crowds of people who gathered on village greens and in city squares. Newspapers also reprinted the document. In Boston, the townspeople rejoiced when the Declaration was read from the balcony of the Old State House. Abigail Adams wrote "The bells rang . . . the cannons were discharged . . . and every face appeared joyful."

Great debate followed with strong arguments being made for and against independence. At first, Pennsylvania and South Carolina voted against independence. But by July 2, every colony voted for independence except New York, which abstained.

By July 4, the Declaration of Independence, which was written mostly by Thomas Jefferson, was ready to be presented. John read it aloud to the Congress. He then signed it with a large and easily read signature. According to legend, John said, as he signed, "There! John Bull [a nickname for Great Britain] can read my name without spectacles and may now double his reward to 500 pounds on my head. That is my defiance." The simple act of signing this document took great courage. It made John a traitor to Britain, which meant that he could be hanged. He was the only man to sign that day. Many signed the next day, but the last of the delegates would not sign their names until

When John Hancock signed the Declaration of Independence, he did so in huge handwriting and added a fancy flourish underneath. John had taken many lessons in handwriting when he was a child. As a result, he wrote beautifully. Today the term "John Hancock" has entered the American vocabulary as a slang expression, meaning one's signature.

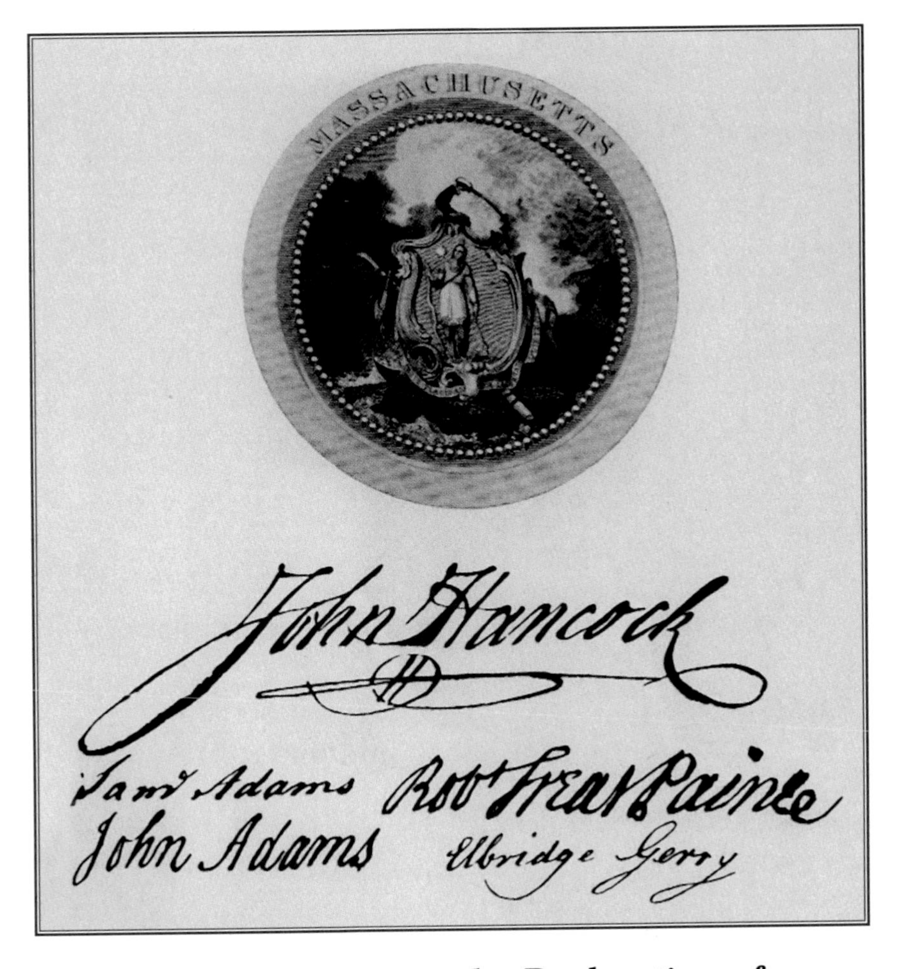

John's signature on the Declaration of Independence was much larger than the others. All five signers from the Massachusetts colony were graduates of Harvard.

November, some four months later.

Recognizing that signing the Declaration of Independence had made them all traitors against Britain, the members of Congress returned to work with a renewed commitment to their purpose–freedom from Britain.

On August 23, King George III formally declared war on the American colonies. That fall John and Dolly became parents to a daughter whose name, unfortunately, is lost to history. When British troops approached Philadelphia, Congress moved to Baltimore, and so did John, taking along a tremendous pile of important papers.

In Baltimore, John and his growing family could only find a house in a bad neighborhood. Thieves broke in and stole clothing, papers, and money. After Washington triumphed in the battles of Trenton and Princeton and pushed the British back from Philadelphia, spirits rose a bit. Congress could go back to Philadelphia, the largest city in America at that time. John left his family in Baltimore for a time to go with the other members of Congress. Dolly also returned to Philadelphia to be with John, but she did not stay. Instead she continued on home to Boston.

In the summer, their baby girl died. John felt very tired and sad.

In the fall, Washington was defeated at Brandywine Creek. Congress had to leave Philadelphia once again. In October, Congress got the news that the American General Horatio Gates had defeated the British army in New York. John decided that this was such good news that he took a leave of absence from Congress. He made a triumphal arrival in Boston on November 19, 1777.

John's mansion on Beacon Hill in Boston. Visitors to Boston can still see many beautiful and historic houses on Beacon Hill.

The End

By the time John returned to Boston in the winter of 1777, the town was in sad shape. Empty shops lined once-busy streets. Many of his friends and neighbors had left to join the Continental Army. Few ships were at anchor in the harbor. John's wharf, though, hummed with activity, because he had government contracts.

His mansion on Beacon Hill looked much as he remembered it. Dolly had been living there. She and John's business manager, William Bant, and two groundskeepers had seen to it that all was in good order. Bant had collected some debts owed

John, even though he was only able to get just a tiny fraction of what people owed. By this time, John didn't own any ships and he was no longer a merchant, because he couldn't import any goods to sell. He did still buy and sell land, and some of the real estate he owned brought in rents. He went over the financial records with Bant. John seems to have been pleased with what Bant was managing to do for him: he decided to leave his business in Bant's hands and devote his time to politics.

In 1777, for the first time in years, John was not elected a selectman for Boston. He was reelected to the Massachusetts legislature, although he did not win by as wide a margin as he had in the past. His former friends, the Adamses, said many unkind things about him.

But in Boston, John still commanded great respect. He used his significant wealth to help many needy people, buying wood for the old folks' home and giving money to widows, orphans, and families whose fathers had gone off to fight in the war. People loved him for his selfless generosity. On December 4, he was reelected as a delegate to the Continental Congress. Soon after, he was also elected moderator of the town meetings.

A group of politicians was then writing a new **constitution** for Massachusetts. John wanted the job of governor, but he did not say so in public. As a member of the legislature, he would have to help write the state constitution. He did not want to be accused of creating a post for himself.

In February 1778, the convention approved the constitution and sent it out to all of the Massachusetts towns for **ratification**. But the voters overwhelmingly rejected it. So there was no race for governor. John decided he would go and take his seat in the Continental Congress. But he did not leave right away. Instead he stayed until May 21, the day that Dolly gave birth to a son, whom they named John George Washington Hancock.

John left in early June, and headed for the Second Continental Congress, which was convening in York, Pennsylvania. While he was gone, the other delegates had elected a new president, so he became just another member of the delegation from Massachusetts. Soon after John arrived in York, the British abandoned Philadelphia, and so Congress moved back there. John went along, but within a month he decided to go home to Boston. He missed his wife and newborn son.

One thing he did before he left Philadelphia was head up a delegation sent to meet the first French minister to the United States, Conrad Alexandre Gerard. France had agreed to join the war against Britain, on the American side. At first, they had planned to attack the British in New York City. But the French ships were unable to enter the harbor, so they decided instead to drive the British out of Newport, Rhode Island.

George Washington sent two brigades to

join in the fight. John went as the commander of the 5,000 Massachusetts militia soldiers who would also fight in the battle. The French ships got caught in a big thunderstorm, and some of them also came under fire by British ships. By the time the remaining ships got to Newport, the French commander had decided not to fight, but to sail to Boston instead. Without naval support, the Americans gave up the idea of a battle. Disappointed, John and his brave Massachusetts militia went home without seeing any action.

By the time John and his men returned to Boston, the French fleet had already arrived. The Hancocks, like other rich Bostonians, entertained French officers every day despite the fact John suffered terribly from gout. Some days he could not even get out of bed. He was irritable. In the poorer part of town, things did not always go well between French sailors and regular folks. Finally, the French left and John threw a final lavish banquet for the French officers.

A new constitutional convention began meeting in Massachusetts on September 1, 1779. John was the convention's speaker and head. He was also reelected to the Continental Congress. On June 16, 1780, the people of Massachusetts ratified their new state constitution, and it went into effect October 25. The election of the governor took place in the fall. John won in a landslide–beating his opponent by a wide margin.

John's inauguration was grand. He arrived in a yellow coach led by marching cadets, and wore a crimson velvet waistcoat with gold trim. After the ceremonies were over, John immediately went back to work. He let the state's legislature handle many of the difficult issues, while he concentrated his efforts on making sure Massachusetts contributed its share of men into the Continental Army.

On October 19, 1781, General Charles Cornwallis surrendered his British army to General George Washington at Yorktown, Virginia. Boston received the news with great

The British army, under General Cornwallis, surrenders to General Washington at Yorktown, Virginia. This event marked the end of the Revolutionary War.

joy and celebration. The fighting was over and the final peace treaty would soon follow.

In the period right after the war, John's business affairs remained in disarray. He also suffered from loneliness for he had few friends left in political circles. Still, he easily won reelection as governor in each of the next four years. By 1785 Massachusetts was suffering from a poor economy. Fishing and shipbuilding had yet to recover from the war. Britain refused to trade with Americans, which hurt local merchants terribly. Some citizens complained bitterly. They did not like John and other rich men like him continuing to throw fancy parties while they suffered. John realized he was not likely to be elected again, and so he resigned his office that year before his term was completed.

Out of office, John tended to his health. He also made some investments in a bridge across the Charles River and in land in Connecticut. In January 1787, John and Dolly Hancock suffered another tragedy, when their son went skating on a pond, fell through the ice, and drowned. Their sadness that winter was overwhelming.

In the spring, to his surprise, John was reelected governor. In May, a convention to draw up a new national government got underway in Philadelphia. As governor, John was sent a copy of the plan for the new government, called the Constitution after it was approved by the convention's delegates.

Before the new government could go into effect, however, at least 9 of the 13 states would have to approve, or ratify, the Constitution.

John called a joint session of the Senate and House of Massachusetts and presented them with the new Constitution. When the state held its ratification convention, John, who went as a delegate from Boston, was elected its president. But he spent little time in his chair due to his ill health.

For a time, it looked like Massachusetts would not vote in favor of the Constitution. But in the end, John spoke out supporting it. Historians say that if John had not helped the cause, Massachusetts and other states might not have ratified this very important document. His action made him popular. He was suggested as a candidate for vice president but did not win the office.

John remained governor of Massachusetts until he died on October 8, 1793. He had been sick for years, even though he was a relatively young man. Summing up his final years, historian William Fowler wrote, "He had sacrificed his

Order of Proceſſion,

for the FUNERAL of the late

GOVERNOR HANCOCK.

FUNERAL ESCORT,
under the Command of
BRIGADIER-GENERAL HULL.

OFFICERS of the MILITIA with ſide Arms,
JUSTICES of the PEACE,
JUDGES of PROBATE,
JUSTICES of the COURT of COMMON PLEAS,
ATTORNEY-GENERAL and TREASURER,
JUSTICES of the SUPREME JUDICIAL COURT,
MEMBERS of the HOUSE of REPRESENTATIVES,
MEMBERS of the SENATE,
SHERIFF of SUFFOLK, with his Wand,
MEMBERS of the COUNCIL,

Quarter M. Gen. / Adjt. General. { HIS HONOR THE LIEUTENANT-GOVERNOR, } Secretary.

This newspaper article announced John's death. He was governor of Massachusetts at the time of his passing.

health, family, and business in America's cause." He was buried in Boston, in the same cemetery as fellow Revolutionary War leaders Paul Revere and Samuel Adams. Today his name remains recognized by virtually all Americans.

GLOSSARY

ancestor–person from whom one is descended

apprentice–a person learning a trade from a skilled worker

casualty–a person injured or killed in a battle

colony–a territory that is settled and governed by the people of another country

condemn–to blame

constitution–a document that states the fundamental principles by which a country is governed

duty–a tax on import goods

effigy–a dummy painted to resemble a hated person

legislature–the branch of a government that makes laws

mansion–a very large and elegant house

merchant–a business person who buys and sells goods

mother country–the country that governs a colony

Parliament–the supreme legislative body of Great Britain

patriot–someone who loves his or her country and supports it

potash–wood ash, used in soap, fertilizers, etc.

ratification–the process a group uses to approve a document

real estate–land or property

rescind–to repeal or do away with a law

theology–studies of God or religions

CHRONOLOGY

1737 Born on January 12 in Braintree, Massachusetts.

1744 Father dies; family moves in with John's grandparents.

1745 Sent to Boston to live with his Uncle Thomas and Aunt Lydia.

1750 Enrolls in Harvard College.

1754 Graduates from college; goes into business with his uncle.

1764 Takes over his uncle's business after Thomas Hancock's death.

1765 Elected a selectman for the town of Boston and begins his political career.

1768 Charged with smuggling after British officials seize the *Liberty*.

1774 Cuts his last ties with British government, resigning from the Massachusetts Corps of Cadets.

1775 Elected president of the Second Continental Congress; marries Dolly Quincy.

1776 Becomes the first to sign the Declaration of Independence on July 4; leaves the Continental Congress and returns to Boston.

1780 Elected governor of Massachusetts for the first of five terms.

1785 Resigns from the office of governor of Massachusetts.

1787 Elected governor of Massachusetts again.

1793 Dies on October 8.

REVOLUTIONARY WAR TIME LINE

1765 The Stamp Act is passed by the British. Violent protests against it break out in the colonies.

1766 Britain ends the Stamp Act.

1767 Britain passes a law that taxes glass, painter's lead, paper, and tea in the colonies.

1770 Five colonists are killed by British soldiers in the Boston Massacre.

1773 People are angry about the taxes on tea. They throw boxes of tea from ships in Boston Harbor into the water. It ruins the tea. The event is called the Boston Tea Party.

1774 The British pass laws to punish Boston for the Boston Tea Party. They close Boston Harbor. Leaders in the colonies meet to plan a response to these actions.

1775 The Battles of Lexington and Concord begin the American Revolution.

1776 The Declaration of Independence is signed. France and Spain give money to help the Americans fight Britain. Nathan Hale is captured by the British. He is charged with being a spy and is executed.

1777 Leaders choose a flag for America. The American troops win some important battles over the British. General Washington and his troops spend a very cold, hungry winter in Valley Forge.

1778 France sends ships to help the Americans win the war. The British are forced to leave Philadelphia.

1779 French ships head back to France. The French support the Americans in other ways.

1780 Americans discover that Benedict Arnold is a traitor. He escapes to the British. Major battles take place in North and South Carolina.

1781 The British surrender at Yorktown.

1783 A peace treaty is signed in France. British troops leave New York.

1787 The U.S. Constitution is written. Delaware becomes the first state in the Union.

1789 George Washington becomes the first president. John Adams is vice president.

FURTHER READING

Dolan, Edward F. *The American Revolution: How We Fought the War of Independence.* Brookfield, Conn.: Millbrook Press, 1995.

Fleming, Thomas. *The First Stroke: Lexington, Concord, and the Beginning of the American Revolution.* Washington, D.C.: National Park Service, 1978.

Fowler, William J. *The Baron of Beacon Hill: A Biography of John Hancock.* Boston: Houghton Mifflin, 1980.

Fradin, Dennis. *Samuel Adams: The Father of American Independence.* New York: Clarion Books, 1998.

O'Neill, Laurie. *The Boston Tea Party.* Brookfield, Conn.: Millbrook Press, 1996.

Quiri, Patricia Ryon. *The Declaration of Independence.* New York: Children's Press, 1998.

INDEX

PICTURE CREDITS

page
3: The Library of Congress
6: The Library of Congress
9: The Library of Congress
13: New Millennium Images
14: The Library of Congress
19: New Millennium Images
23: National Archives
25: National Archives
28: National Archives
32: The Library of Congress
39: National Archives
41: National Archives
42: The Library of Congress
47: National Archives
48: National Archives
51: National Archives
53: New Millennium Images
56: New Millennium Images
59: The Library of Congress
62: New Millennium Images
69: New Millennium Images
72: The Library of Congress

ABOUT THE AUTHOR

ANN GRAHAM GAINES is a freelance author and photo researcher who lives in the woods near Gonzales, Texas, with her four children.

Senior Consulting Editor **ARTHUR M. SCHLESINGER, JR.** is the leading American historian of our time. He won the Pulitzer Prize for his book *The Age of Jackson* (1945), and again for *A Thousand Days* (1965). This chronicle of the Kennedy Administration also won a National Book Award. He has written many other books, including a multi-volume series, *The Age of Roosevelt.* Professor Schlesinger is the Albert Schweitzer Professor of the Humanities at the City University of New York, and has been involved in several other Chelsea House projects, including the COLONIAL LEADERS series of biographies on the most prominent figures of early American history.